UNDER WATER WITH OGDEN NASH

UNDER WATER WITH OGDEN NASH

OGDEN NASH

ILLUSTRATIONS BY KATIE LEE

A Bulfinch Press Book
Little, Brown and Company
Boston • New York • Toronto • London

First Edition

Library of Congress Cataloging-in-Publication Data
Nash, Ogden, 1902-1971.
    Under water with Ogden Nash/by Ogden Nash: illustrations by
Katie Lee.—1st ed.
        p. cm.
    "A Bulfinch Press book."
    ISBN 0-8212-2404-2
    1. Marine fauna—Poetry. 2. Humorous poetry, American.
    I. Title.
    PS3527.A637U53 1997
    811'.52—dc21   96-51448

Bulfinch Press is an imprint and trademark of Little, Brown and Company (Inc.)
Published simultaneously in Canada by Little, Brown & Company (Canada) Limited

Design by Sherry Fatla

PRINTED IN SINGAPORE

FOR SUSAN

❧ CONTENTS ❧

Some fish are minnows,
Some are whales.
People like dimples,
Fish like scales.
Some fish are slim,
And some are round.
Fish don't get cold,
And don't get drowned.
But every fish wife
Is jealous for her fish
Of what we call mermaids,
And they call merfish.

THE SHRIMP

A shrimp who sought his lady shrimp
Could catch no glimpse,
Not even a glimp.
At times, translucence
Is rather a nuisance.

THE FISH

The fish, when he's exposed to air,
Displays no trace of *savoir-faire*,
But in the sea regains his balance
And exploits all his manly talents.
The chastest of the vertebrates,
He never even sees his mates,
But when they've finished, he appears
And O.K.'s all their bright ideas.

❦ THE TURTLE ❦

The turtle lives 'twixt plated decks
Which practically conceal its sex.
I think it clever of the turtle
In such a fix to be so fertile.

❧ THE PORPOISE ❧

I kind of like the playful porpoise,
A healthy mind in a healthy corpus.
He and his cousin, the playful dolphin,
Why they like swimmin like I like golphin.

❧ THE CLAM ❧

The clam, esteemed by gourmets highly,
Is said to live the life of Riley;
When you are lolling on a piazza
It's what you are as happy as a.

❧ THE MANATEE ❧

The manatee is harmless
And conspicuously charmless.
Luckily the manatee
Is quite devoid of vanity.

THE SEA-GULL

Hark to the whimper of the sea-gull;
He weeps because he's not an ea-gull.
Suppose you were, you silly sea-gull,
Could you explain it to your she-gull?

≈ THE MERMAID ≈

Say not the mermaid is a myth,
I knew one once named Mrs. Smith.
She stood while playing cards or knitting;
Mermaids are not equipped for sitting.

THE HIPPOPOTAMUS

Behold the hippopotamus!
We laugh at how he looks to us,
And yet in moments dank and grim
I wonder how we look to him.
Peace, peace, thou hippopotamus!
We really look all right to us,
As you no doubt delight the eye
Of other hippopotami.

A giant new prawn has been dredged up near Santiago, Chile . . . it is
succulent and mysterious. . . . The new prawn has not been named, a
fact that is causing no concern in Chile.—TIMES

Could some descending escalator

Deposit me below the equator,

I'd hunt me a quiet Chilean haunt,

Some Santiago restaurant;

The fact I speak no *Español*

Would handicap me not at all,

Since any language would be aimless

In ordering a tidbit nameless;

I'd simply tie my napkin on

And gesture like a giant prawn,

Then, served the dish for which I yearned,

Proceed to munch it, unconcerned.

Happy crustacean, anonymous prawn,

from distant Latin waters drawn,

Hadst thou in Yankee seas appeared,

Account executives would have cheered,

Vice-presidents in paroxysms
Accorded thee multiple baptisms;
Yea, shouldst thou hit our markets now,
Soon, prawn, wouldst thou be named—and how!
I see the bright ideas drawn:
Prawno, Prawnex, and Vitaprawn;
And, should upper-bracket dreamers wake,
Squab o' Neptune, and Plankton Steak.
Small wonder thou headest for Santiago,
Where gourmets ignore such frantic farrago;
That's exactly where I myself would have went if I'd
Been mysterious, succulent, unidentified.

❧ THE JELLYFISH ❧

Who wants my jellyfish?
I'm not sellyfish!

❧ THE PLATYPUS ❧

I like the duck-billed platypus
Because it is anomalous.
I like the way it raises its family,
Partly birdly, partly mammaly.
I like its independent attitude.
Let no one call it a duck-billed platitude.

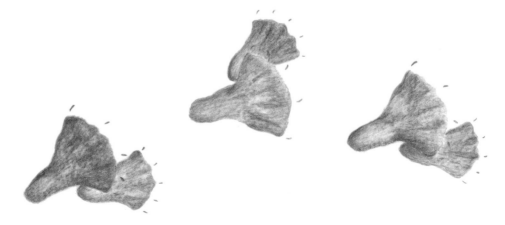

THE GANDER

Be careful not to cross the gander,
A bird composed of beak and dander.
His heart is filled with prideful hate
Of all the world except his mate,
And if the neighbors do not err
He's overfond of beating her.
Is she happy? What's the use
Of trying to psychoanalyze a goose?

❧ THE SWAN ❧

Scholars call the masculine swan a cob;
I call him a narcissistic snob.
He looks in the mirror over and over,
And claims to have never heard of Pavlova.

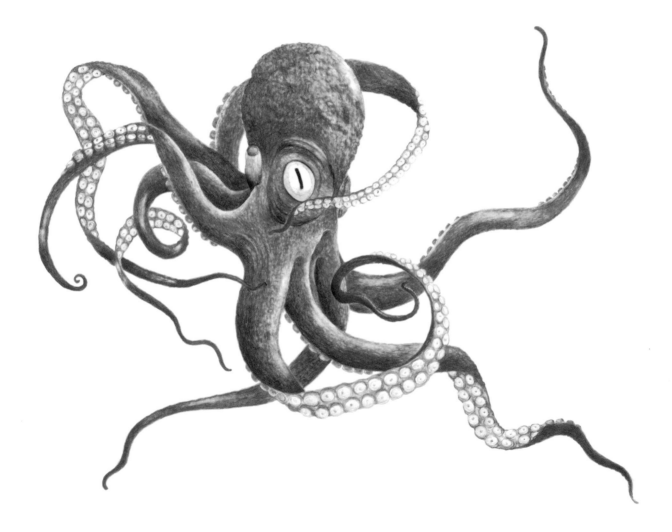

❧ THE OCTOPUS ❧

Tell me, O Octopus, I begs,
Is those things arms, or is they legs?
I marvel at thee, Octopus;
If I were thou, I'd call me Us.

❧ THE SHAD ❧

I'm sure that Europe never had
A fish as tasty as the shad.
Some people greet the shad with groans,
Complaining of its countless bones;

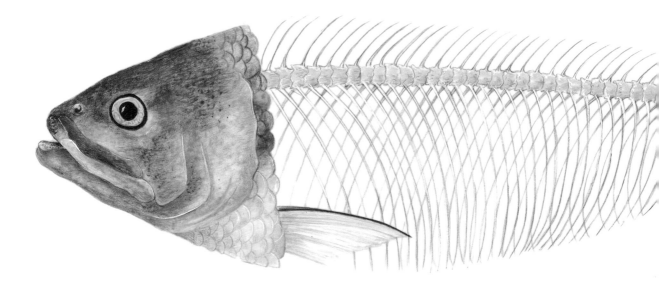

I claim the bones teach table poise
And separate the men from boys.
The shad must be dissected subtle-y;
Besides, the roe is boneless, utterly.

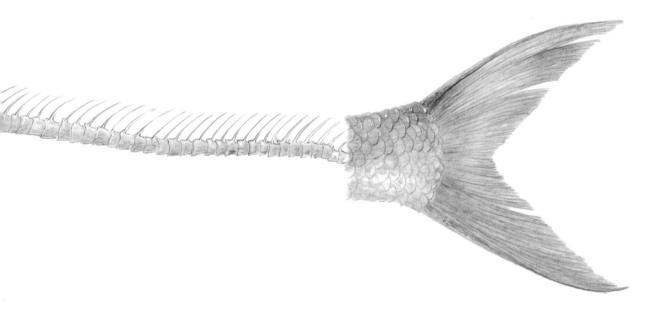

❧ THE SHARK ❧

How many Scientists have written
The shark is gentle as a kitten!
Yet this I know about the shark:
His bite is worser than his bark.

❧ BARMAIDS ARE DIVINER THAN MERMAIDS ❧

Fish are very good at swimming,

And the ocean with them is brimming.

They stay under water all year round,

And they never get drowned,

And they have a gift more precious than gold,

Which is that they never get cold.

No, they may not be as tasty as venison or mooseflesh,

But they never get gooseflesh.

They have been in the ocean since they were roe,

So they don't have to creep into it toe by toe,

And also they stay in it permanently, which must be a source of
    great satisfaction,

Because they don't have to run dripping and shivering up and
    down the beach waiting vainly for a healthy reaction.

Indeed when I think how uncomplicated the ocean is for fish my
    thoughts grow jealous and scathing,

Because when fish bump into another fish it doesn't wring from
    them a cry of Faugh! and ruin their day's bathing.

No, if it's a bigger fish than they are, they turn around and beat it,

And if it's littler, they eat it.

Some fish are striped and some are speckled,

But none of them ever heard of ultra-violet rays and felt it necessary
to lie around getting sand in their eyes and freckled.

Oh, would it not be wondrous to be a fish? No, it would not be
wondrous,

Because we unmarine humans are at the top of the animal kingdom
and it would be very undignified to change places with
anything under us.

THE LAMPREY

Lampreys are hagfish. In that one word I've said it.
I only know one item to their credit.
The early English had good cause to love them;
Wicked King John died from a surfeit of them.

THE OYSTER

The oyster's a confusing suitor;
It's masc., and fem., and even neuter.
At times it wonders, may what come,
Am I husband, wife, or chum.

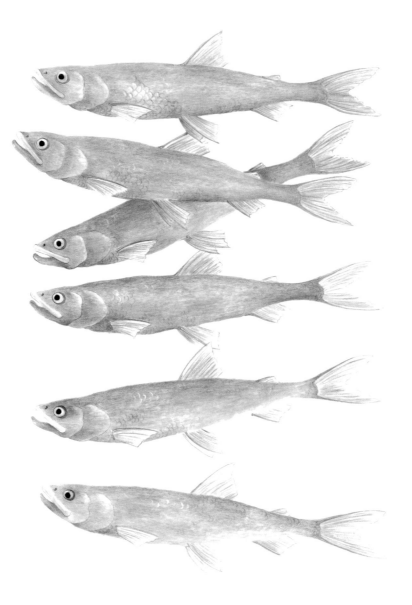

❧ THE SMELT ❧

Oh, why does man pursue the smelt?

It has no valuable pelt,

It boasts of no escutcheon royal,

It yields no ivory or oil,

Its life is dull, its death is tame,

A fish as humble as its name.

Yet—take this salmon somewhere else,

And bring me half a dozen smelts.

❧ THE EEL ❧

I don't mind eels
Except as meals.

❧ THE PURIST ❧

I give you now Professor Twist,
A conscientious scientist,
Trustees exclaimed, 'He never bungles!'
And sent him off to distant jungles.
Camped on a tropic riverside,
One day he missed his loving bride.
She had, the guide informed him later,
Been eaten by an alligator.
Professor Twist could not but smile.
'You mean,' he said, 'a crocodile.'

❧ THE SQUID ❧

What happy appellations these
Of birds and beasts in companies!
A shrewdness of apes, a sloth of bears,
A sculk of foxes, a huske of hares.
An exaltation 'tis of larks,
And possibly a grin of sharks,
But I declare a squirt of squid
I should not like to be amid,
Though bachelors claim that a cloud of sepia
Makes a splendid hiding place in Leap Year.

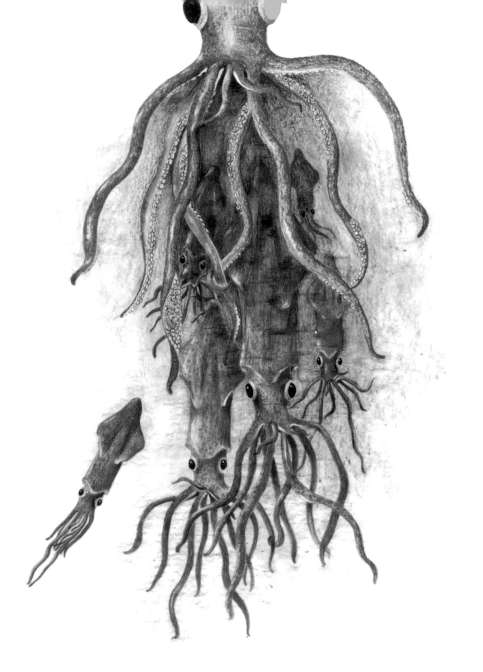

❧ THE GUPPY ❧

Whales have calves,
Cats have kittens,
Bears have cubs,
Bats have bittens.
Swans have cygnets,
Seals have puppies,
But guppies just have little guppies.

❧ THE DUCK ❧

Behold the duck.

It does not cluck.

A cluck it lacks.

It quacks.

It is specially fond

Of a puddle or a pond.

When it dines or sups,

It bottoms ups.

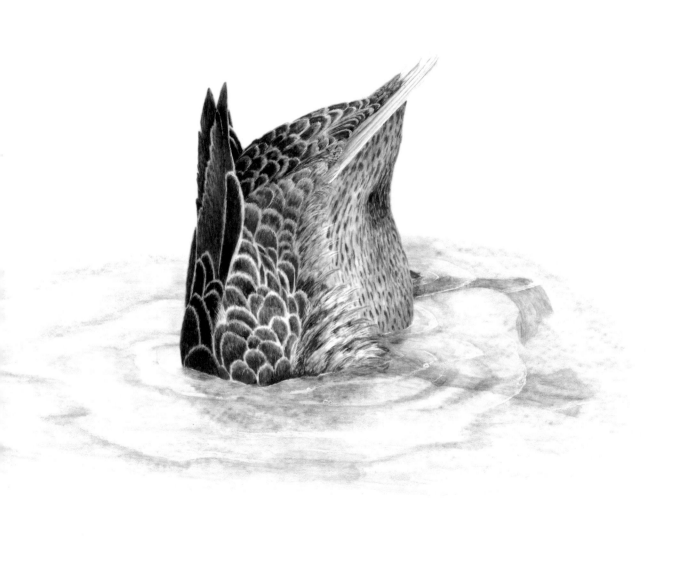